THIS BOOK BELONGS TO

_____

START DATE

_____

SHE READS TRUTH

EXECUTIVE

FOUNDER/CHIEF EXECUTIVE OFFICER
Raechel Myers

CO-FOUNDER/CHIEF CONTENT OFFICER
Amanda Bible Williams

CHIEF OPERATING OFFICER
Ryan Myers

EXECUTIVE ASSISTANT
Sarah Andereck

EDITORIAL

EDITORIAL DIRECTOR
Jessica Lamb

MANAGING EDITOR
Beth Joseph

CONTENT EDITOR
Kara Gause

ASSOCIATE EDITORS
Bailey Gillespie
Tameshia Williams

EDITORIAL ASSISTANT
Hannah Little

CREATIVE

CREATIVE DIRECTOR
Jeremy Mitchell

LEAD DESIGNER
Kelsea Allen

DESIGNERS
Abbey Benson
Davis DeLisi
Annie Glover

MARKETING

MARKETING DIRECTOR
Krista Juline Wharton

MARKETING MANAGER
Katie Matuska Pierce

COMMUNITY SUPPORT SPECIALIST
Margot Williams

SHIPPING & LOGISTICS

LOGISTICS MANAGER
Lauren Gloyne

CUSTOMER SUPPORT SPECIALIST
Katy McKnight

FULFILLMENT LEAD
Abigail Achord

FULFILLMENT SPECIALISTS
Cait Baggerman
Noe Sanchez

SUBSCRIPTION INQUIRIES
orders@shereadstruth.com

@SHEREADSTRUTH

Download the
She Reads Truth app,
available for iOS
and Android

Subscribe to the
She Reads Truth podcast

SHEREADSTRUTH.COM

This book was printed offset in Nashville, Tennessee, on 70# Lynx Opaque. Cover is 100# Cougar Opaque with a soft touch lamination.

THE KINGDOM OF GOD

We are here in this imperfect place on purpose and for a purpose; we are part of God's plan to bring His kingdom to bear on earth.

Amanda

Amanda Bible Williams
CO-FOUNDER & CHIEF
CONTENT OFFICER

This world is not our home.

It's a statement I've heard, and even said, often in my years of growing up in the Church and following Jesus. Sometimes it's offered as a lament, acknowledging the brokenness and flaws inherent in this earthly life. Other times it's meant as encouragement, reminding us of the joy and perfection of the eternal life to come. Either way, it testifies to a sort of emptiness, a restlessness—that nagging feeling of incompleteness common to the human experience. C.S. Lewis said it this way in his book *Mere Christianity*: "If I find in myself a desire which no experience in this world can satisfy, the most probable explanation is that I was made for another world."

And he's right. Scripture teaches that the world cannot fill our God-shaped longings. "I desire nothing on earth but you," the psalmist cries out (Psalm 73:25). We were made to be in perfect fellowship with God, our Creator, and that perfection is not something we will know until every tear is wiped away and all things are made new. But Scripture also makes it clear that we are here in this imperfect place on purpose and for a purpose; we are part of God's plan to bring His kingdom to bear on earth. We are written into His redemption story.

So, what does that mean for right here and right now? How do we live on earth as citizens of heaven? What does it look like to embrace the already-and-not-yet reality of our permanent home—the kingdom of God—while here in our temporary one?

In the first part of this three-week study, we will look to Scripture to better understand Jesus, the King, and the nature of the kingdom of God. Then we'll spend the remaining two weeks reading about life in the kingdom. Who are its citizens? What are its values, law, and purpose? What does it mean to enter into the kingdom of God while also anticipating it? How does King Jesus call us to live?

Throughout this Study Book, you'll have the opportunity to reflect on what you're learning about God's kingdom through unique questions for each day's reading. You'll also get to dig deeper into specific passages and concepts with charts like "Jesus Interprets the Law" on page 78 and "The Kingdom of God in the Old Testament" on page 110. Above all, you'll be invited to consider the reality of the ultimate kingdom and the forever King.

By God's grace, may this reality rekindle our passion for following Jesus, as we submit every corner of our hearts and lives to His rule. May we "press on to that other country," as Lewis said, and "help others to do the same." This is, after all, what we were made for.

PANTONE®
7527 U

PANTONE®
7530 U

ABCDEFGHIJ
KLMNOPQRS
TUVWXYZ
0123456789

At She Reads Truth, we believe in pairing the inherently beautiful Word of God with the aesthetic beauty it deserves. Each of our resources is thoughtfully and artfully designed to highlight the beauty, goodness, and truth of Scripture in a way that reflects the themes of each curated reading plan.

For this Study Book, we chose images taken with a macro camera lens to showcase subjects in a new, abstract perspective. This more intimate look at something familiar is reminiscent of how a kingdom perspective changes how we see the world around us.

HOW TO USE THIS BOOK

She Reads Truth is a community of women dedicated
to reading the Word of God every day. The Bible is
living and active, and we confidently hold it higher
than anything we can do or say.

READ & REFLECT

The Kingdom of God Study Book
focuses primarily on Scripture, with
bonus resources to facilitate deeper
engagement with God's Word.

SCRIPTURE READING

Designed for a Monday start,
this Study Book presents daily
readings on the kingdom of God.

REFLECTION

Each weekday features questions
for personal reflection.

COMMUNITY & CONVERSATION

Join women from Clackamas to Canada as they
read with you!

 SHE READS TRUTH APP

Devotionals corresponding to each daily reading
can be found in **The Kingdom of God** reading plan on
the She Reads Truth app. You can also participate in
community discussions, download free lock screens
for Weekly Truth memorization, and more.

GRACE DAY

Use Saturdays to catch up on your reading, pray, and rest in the presence of the Lord.

WEEKLY TRUTH

Sundays are set aside for Scripture memorization.

EXTRAS

This book features additional tools to help you gain a deeper understanding of the text.

See a complete list of extras on page 11.

 SHEREADSTRUTH.COM

All of our reading plans and devotionals are also available at SheReadsTruth.com. Invite your family, friends, and neighbors to read along with you!

 SHE READS TRUTH PODCAST

Join our She Reads Truth founders and their guests each Monday as they open their Bibles and talk about the beauty, goodness, and truth they find there. Each podcast episode corresponds to the current community reading plan. Subscribe on your favorite podcast app so you don't miss a conversation about **The Kingdom of God** and more.

TABLE OF CONTENTS

Week 01

Day 01	The Forever King	p. 16
Day 02	The Kingdom Is Here	p. 25
Day 03	The Reign of the King	p. 32
Day 04	The Nature of the Kingdom	p. 39
Day 05	The Kingdom Is Coming	p. 46
Day 06	Grace Day	p. 54
Day 07	Weekly Truth	p. 56

Week 02

Day 08	The King's People	p. 61
Day 09	The Kingdom Is Theirs	p. 66
Day 10	The Law of the Kingdom	p. 73
Day 11	God's Kingdom Come	p. 80
Day 12	Treasures of the Kingdom	p. 89
Day 13	Grace Day	p. 94
Day 14	Weekly Truth	p. 96

Week O3

Day 15	Entering the Kingdom	p. 98
Day 16	Anticipating the Kingdom	p. 105
Day 17	Allegiance to the King	p. 115
Day 18	Advancing the Kingdom	p. 122
Day 19	The Fullness of the Kingdom	p. 128
Day 20	Grace Day	p. 136
Day 21	Weekly Truth	p. 138

EXTRAS

Handel's *Messiah*: "Hallelujah Chorus"	p. 12
Section 1 Introduction	p. 14
What Is a Parable?	p. 52
Section 2 Introduction	p. 58
Jesus Interprets the Law	p. 78
The Kingdom of God in the Old Testament	p. 110
Benediction	p. 140
For the Record	p. 144

HANDEL'S MESSIAH:

"Hallelujah Chorus"

Seated among classic works in the unique genre of *oratoria*, George Frideric Handel's *Messiah* is a dramatic telling of the events of Jesus's life, death, and resurrection. A long-time Christmas classic that was originally intended as an Easter offering, this renowned composition extends far beyond the Advent and Lent seasons, celebrating that Jesus Christ is the true, divine Messiah—the Son of God.

The "Hallelujah Chorus" is a movement within Handel's *Messiah*, shown here and featured throughout this book that is inspired by the book of Revelation. These lyrics are a hopeful reminder that God's kingdom will reign forever and ever.

HALLELUJAH!
FOR THE LORD
GOD OMNIPOTENT
REIGNETH.

THE KINGDOM OF THIS
WORLD IS BECOME
THE KINGDOM OF
OUR LORD,
AND OF HIS CHRIST:

AND HE SHALL REIGN
FOREVER AND EVER.
KING OF KINGS,
LORD OF LORDS.

THE ALREADY-AND-NOT-YET KINGDOM OF GOD

Like the early Church, we exist in the tension of the already-and-not-yet nature of the kingdom of God. Jesus inaugurated this kingdom, bringing reconciling peace to earth through His life, death, and resurrection, and ushering in the beginning of the renewal of all things. But God's kingdom will only be fully and finally established at the return of Christ. While Christ reigns as our perfect King, we are still waiting for the kingdom to come in full.

In the first week of this study, we will discover who Jesus is and what His kingdom and reign look like.

Jesus came as the perfect, eternal King.

THE FOREVER KING

2 Samuel 7:8–16

[8] "So now this is what you are to say to my servant David: 'This is what the LORD of Armies says: I took you from the pasture, from tending the flock, to be ruler over my people Israel. [9] I have been with you wherever you have gone, and I have destroyed all your enemies before you. I will make a great name for you like that of the greatest on the earth. [10] I will designate a place for my people Israel and plant them, so that they may live there and not be disturbed again. Evildoers will not continue to oppress them as they have done [11] ever since the day I ordered judges to be over my people Israel. I will give you rest from all your enemies.

"'The LORD declares to you: The LORD himself will make a house for you. [12] When your time comes and you rest with your ancestors, I will raise up after you your descendant, who will come from your body, and I will establish his kingdom. [13] He is the one who will build a house for my name, and I will establish the throne of his kingdom forever. [14] I will be his father, and he will be my son. When he does wrong, I will discipline him with a rod of men and blows from mortals. [15] But my faithful love will never leave him as it did when I removed it from Saul, whom I removed from before you. [16] Your house and kingdom will endure before me forever, and your throne will be established forever.'"

Luke 2:1–20

THE BIRTH OF JESUS

[1] In those days a decree went out from Caesar Augustus that the whole empire should be registered. [2] This first registration took place while Quirinius was governing Syria. [3] So everyone went to be registered, each to his own town.

[4] Joseph also went up from the town of Nazareth in Galilee, to Judea, to the city of David, which is called Bethlehem, because he was of the house and family line of David, [5] to be registered along with Mary, who was engaged to him and was pregnant. [6] While they were there, the time came for her to give birth. [7] Then she gave birth to her firstborn son, and she wrapped him tightly in cloth and laid him in a manger, because there was no guest room available for them.

THE SHEPHERDS AND THE ANGELS

[8] In the same region, shepherds were staying out in the fields and keeping watch at night over their flock. [9] Then an angel of the Lord stood before them, and the glory of the Lord shone around them, and they were terrified. [10] But the angel said to them, "Don't be afraid, for look, I proclaim to you good news of great joy that will be for all the people: [11] Today in the city of David a Savior was born for you, who is the Messiah, the Lord. [12] This will be the sign for you: You will find a baby wrapped tightly in cloth and lying in a manger."

[13] Suddenly there was a multitude of the heavenly host with the angel, praising God and saying:

> [14] Glory to God in the highest heaven,
> and peace on earth to people he favors!

[15] When the angels had left them and returned to heaven, the shepherds said to one another, "Let's go straight to Bethlehem and see what has happened, which the Lord has made known to us."

[16] They hurried off and found both Mary and Joseph, and the baby who was lying in the manger. [17] After seeing them, they reported the message they were told about this child, [18] and all who heard it were amazed at what the shepherds said to them. [19] But Mary was treasuring up all these things in her heart and meditating on them. [20] The shepherds returned, glorifying and praising God for all the things they had seen and heard, which were just as they had been told.

Matthew 2:1–11

WISE MEN VISIT THE KING

[1] After Jesus was born in Bethlehem of Judea in the days of King Herod, wise men from the east arrived in Jerusalem, [2] saying,

"Where is he who has been born king of the Jews?

For we saw his star at its rising and have come to worship him."

[3] When King Herod heard this, he was deeply disturbed, and all Jerusalem with him. [4] So he assembled all the chief priests and scribes of the people and asked them where the Messiah would be born.

[5] "In Bethlehem of Judea," they told him, "because this is what was written by the prophet:

> [6] And you, Bethlehem, in the land of Judah,
> are by no means least among the rulers of Judah:
> Because out of you will come a ruler
> who will shepherd my people Israel."

[7] Then Herod secretly summoned the wise men and asked them the exact time the star appeared. [8] He sent them to Bethlehem and said, "Go and search carefully for the child. When you find him, report back to me so that I too can go and worship him."

⁹ After hearing the king, they went on their way. And there it was—the star they had seen at its rising. It led them until it came and stopped above the place where the child was. ¹⁰ When they saw the star, they were overwhelmed with joy. ¹¹ Entering the house, they saw the child with Mary his mother, and falling to their knees, they worshiped him. Then they opened their treasures and presented him with gifts: gold, frankincense, and myrrh.

Matthew 21:1–10

THE TRIUMPHAL ENTRY

¹ When they approached Jerusalem and came to Bethphage at the Mount of Olives, Jesus then sent two disciples, ² telling them, "Go into the village ahead of you. At once you will find a donkey tied there with her colt. Untie them and bring them to me. ³ If anyone says anything to you, say that the Lord needs them, and he will send them at once."

⁴ This took place so that what was spoken through the prophet might be fulfilled:

⁵ Tell Daughter Zion,
"See, your King is coming to you,
gentle, and mounted on a donkey,
and on a colt,
the foal of a donkey."

⁶ The disciples went and did just as Jesus directed them. ⁷ They brought the donkey and the colt; then they laid their clothes on them, and he sat on them. ⁸ A very large crowd spread their clothes on the road; others were cutting branches from the trees and spreading them on the road. ⁹ Then the crowds who went ahead of him and those who followed shouted:

Hosanna to the Son of David!
Blessed is he who comes in the name
of the Lord!
Hosanna in the highest heaven!

¹⁰ When he entered Jerusalem, the whole city was in an uproar, saying, "Who is this?"

Acts 2:29–36

²⁹ Brothers and sisters, I can confidently speak to you about the patriarch David: He is both dead and buried, and his tomb is with us to this day. ³⁰ Since he was a prophet, he knew that God had sworn an oath to him to seat one of his

descendants on his throne. [31] Seeing what was to come, he spoke concerning the resurrection of the Messiah: He was not abandoned in Hades, and his flesh did not experience decay.

[32] God has raised this Jesus; we are all witnesses of this. [33] Therefore, since he has been exalted to the right hand of God and has received from the Father the promised Holy Spirit, he has poured out what you both see and hear. [34] For it was not David who ascended into the heavens, but he himself says:

> The Lord declared to my Lord,
> "Sit at my right hand
> [35] until I make your enemies your footstool."

[36] Therefore let all the house of Israel know with certainty that God has made this Jesus, whom you crucified, both Lord and Messiah.

Ephesians 1:20–21

GOD'S POWER IN CHRIST

[20] He exercised this power in Christ by raising him from the dead and seating him at his right hand in the heavens— [21] far above every ruler and authority, power and dominion, and every title given, not only in this age but also in the one to come.

Day 01

REFLECTION

How do the details of Jesus's birth and entry into Jerusalem
show Him to be a different kind of King?

QUESTIONS

According to Acts 2:29–36 and Ephesians 1:20–21, what events marked
Jesus taking the throne? Where is He still?

THE KINGDOM IS HERE

Day 02

God's kingdom came to reign on earth
in a new, decisive way through Jesus.

Daniel 2:31–45

31 Your Majesty, as you were watching, suddenly a colossal statue appeared. That statue, tall and dazzling, was standing in front of you, and its appearance was terrifying. 32 The head of the statue was pure gold, its chest and arms were silver, its stomach and thighs were bronze, 33 its legs were iron, and its feet were partly iron and partly fired clay. 34 As you were watching, a stone broke off without a hand touching it, struck the statue on its feet of iron and fired clay, and crushed them. 35 Then the iron, the fired clay, the bronze, the silver, and the gold were shattered and became like chaff from the summer threshing floors. The wind carried them away, and not a trace of them could be found. But the stone that struck the statue became a great mountain and filled the whole earth.

36 This was the dream; now we will tell the king its interpretation. 37 Your Majesty, you are king of kings. The God of the heavens has given you sovereignty, power, strength, and glory. 38 Wherever people live—or wild animals, or birds of the sky—he has handed them over to you and made you ruler over them all. You are the head of gold.

39 After you, there will arise another kingdom, inferior to yours, and then another, a third kingdom, of bronze, which will rule the whole earth. 40 A fourth kingdom will be as strong as iron; for iron crushes and shatters everything, and like iron that smashes, it will crush and smash all the others. 41 You saw the feet and toes, partly of a potter's fired clay and partly of iron—it will be a divided kingdom, though some

of the strength of iron will be in it. You saw the iron mixed with clay, [42] and that the toes of the feet were partly iron and partly fired clay—part of the kingdom will be strong, and part will be brittle. [43] You saw the iron mixed with clay—the peoples will mix with one another but will not hold together, just as iron does not mix with fired clay.

[44] In the days of those kings, the God of the heavens will set up a kingdom that will never be destroyed, and this kingdom will not be left to another people. It will crush all these kingdoms and bring them to an end, but will itself endure forever. [45] You saw a stone break off from the mountain without a hand touching it, and it crushed the iron, bronze, fired clay, silver, and gold. The great God has told the king what will happen in the future. The dream is certain, and its interpretation reliable.

Matthew 3

THE HERALD OF THE MESSIAH

[1] In those days John the Baptist came, preaching in the wilderness of Judea [2] and saying,

"Repent, because the kingdom of heaven has come near!"

[3] For he is the one spoken of through the prophet Isaiah, who said:

A voice of one crying out in the wilderness:
Prepare the way for the Lord;
make his paths straight!

[4] Now John had a camel-hair garment with a leather belt around his waist, and his food was locusts and wild honey. [5] Then people from Jerusalem, all Judea, and all the vicinity of the Jordan were going out to him, [6] and they were baptized by him in the Jordan River, confessing their sins.

[7] When he saw many of the Pharisees and Sadducees coming to his baptism, he said to them, "Brood of vipers! Who warned you to flee from the coming wrath? [8] Therefore produce fruit consistent with repentance. [9] And don't presume to say to yourselves, 'We have Abraham as our father.' For I tell you that God is able to raise up children for Abraham from these stones. [10] The ax is already at the root of the trees. Therefore, every tree that doesn't produce good fruit will be cut down and thrown into the fire.

[11] "I baptize you with water for repentance, but the one who is coming after me is more powerful than I. I am not worthy to remove his sandals. He himself will

baptize you with the Holy Spirit and fire. [12] His winnowing shovel is in his hand, and he will clear his threshing floor and gather his wheat into the barn. But the chaff he will burn with fire that never goes out."

[13] Then Jesus came from Galilee to John at the Jordan, to be baptized by him. [14] But John tried to stop him, saying, "I need to be baptized by you, and yet you come to me?"

[15] Jesus answered him, "Allow it for now, because this is the way for us to fulfill all righteousness." Then John allowed him to be baptized.

[16] When Jesus was baptized, he went up immediately from the water. The heavens suddenly opened for him, and he saw the Spirit of God descending like a dove and coming down on him. [17] And a voice from heaven said, "This is my beloved Son, with whom I am well-pleased."

John 1:29–34

THE LAMB OF GOD

[29] The next day John saw Jesus coming toward him and said, "Look, the Lamb of God, who takes away the sin of the world! [30] This is the one I told you about: 'After me comes a man who ranks ahead of me, because he existed before me.' [31] I didn't know him, but I came baptizing with water so that he might be revealed to Israel." [32] And John testified, "I saw the Spirit descending from heaven like a dove, and he rested on him. [33] I didn't know him, but he who sent me to baptize with water told me, 'The one you see the Spirit descending and resting on—he is the one who baptizes with the Holy Spirit.' [34] I have seen and testified that this is the Son of God."

John 18:36–37

[36] "My kingdom is not of this world," said Jesus. "If my kingdom were of this world, my servants would fight, so that I wouldn't be handed over to the Jews. But as it is, my kingdom is not from here."

[37] "You are a king then?" Pilate asked.

"You say that I'm a king," Jesus replied. "I was born for this, and I have come into the world for this: to testify to the truth. Everyone who is of the truth listens to my voice."

Day 02

REFLECTION

How does Daniel 2 expand your understanding of John and
Jesus's proclamations about God's kingdom?

QUESTIONS

What does John offer as evidence that
God's kingdom is present now?

HALLELUJAH!

FOR THE LORD GOD OMNIPOTENT REIGNETH.

Handel's *Messiah*: "Hallelujah Chorus"

THE REIGN OF THE KING

Jesus demonstrated His authority as the true Son of God, who now rules at the right hand of the Father.

Daniel 7:13–14

¹³ I continued watching in the night visions,

> and suddenly one like a son of man
> was coming with the clouds of heaven.
> He approached the Ancient of Days
> and was escorted before him.
> ¹⁴ He was given dominion
> and glory and a kingdom,
> so that those of every people,
> nation, and language
> should serve him.
> His dominion is an everlasting dominion
> that will not pass away,
> and his kingdom is one
> that will not be destroyed.

Matthew 28:1–10, 16–18

RESURRECTION MORNING

¹ After the Sabbath, as the first day of the week was dawning, Mary Magdalene and the other Mary went to view the tomb. ² There was a violent earthquake, because an angel of the Lord descended from heaven and approached the tomb. He rolled back the stone and was sitting on it. ³ His appearance was like lightning, and his clothing was as white as snow. ⁴ The guards were so shaken by fear of him that they became like dead men.

⁵ The angel told the women, "Don't be afraid, because I know you are looking for Jesus who was crucified. ⁶ He is not here. For he has risen, just as he said. Come and see the place where he lay. ⁷ Then go quickly and tell his disciples, 'He has risen from the dead and indeed he is going ahead of you to Galilee; you will see him there.' Listen, I have told you."

⁸ So, departing quickly from the tomb with fear and great joy, they ran to tell his disciples the news. ⁹ Just then Jesus met them and said, "Greetings!" They came up, took hold of his feet, and worshiped him. ¹⁰ Then Jesus told them, "Do not be afraid. Go and tell my brothers to leave for Galilee, and they will see me there."

…

THE GREAT COMMISSION

¹⁶ The eleven disciples traveled to Galilee, to the mountain where Jesus had directed them. ¹⁷ When they saw him, they worshiped, but some doubted. ¹⁸ Jesus came near and said to them, "All authority has been given to me in heaven and on earth."

Philippians 2:5–11

CHRIST'S HUMILITY AND EXALTATION

⁵ Adopt the same attitude as that of Christ Jesus,

⁶ who, existing in the form of God,
did not consider equality with God
as something to be exploited.
⁷ Instead he emptied himself
by assuming the form of a servant,
taking on the likeness of humanity.
And when he had come as a man,
⁸ he humbled himself by becoming obedient
to the point of death—
even to death on a cross.
⁹ For this reason God highly exalted him
and gave him the name
that is above every name,
¹⁰ so that at the name of Jesus
every knee will bow—
in heaven and on earth
and under the earth—
¹¹ and every tongue will confess
that Jesus Christ is Lord,
to the glory of God the Father.

Colossians 1:15–23

THE CENTRALITY OF CHRIST

¹⁵ He is the image of the invisible God,
the firstborn over all creation.
¹⁶ For everything was created by him,

in heaven and on earth,
the visible and the invisible,
whether thrones or dominions
or rulers or authorities—
all things have been created through him and for him.
[17] He is before all things,
and by him all things hold together.
[18] He is also the head of the body, the church;
he is the beginning,
the firstborn from the dead,
so that he might come to have
first place in everything.
[19] For God was pleased to have
all his fullness dwell in him,
[20] and through him to reconcile
everything to himself,
whether things on earth or things in heaven,
by making peace
through his blood, shed on the cross.

[21] Once you were alienated and hostile in your minds as expressed in your evil actions. [22] But now he has reconciled you by his physical body through his death, to present you holy, faultless, and blameless before him— [23] if indeed you remain grounded and steadfast in the faith and are not shifted away from the hope of the gospel that you heard. This gospel has been proclaimed in all creation under heaven, and I, Paul, have become a servant of it.

Revelation 19:11–16

THE RIDER ON A WHITE HORSE

[11] Then I saw heaven opened, and there was a white horse. Its rider is called Faithful and True, and with justice he judges and makes war. [12] His eyes were like a fiery flame, and many crowns were on his head. He had a name written that no one knows except himself. [13] He wore a robe dipped in blood, and his name is called the Word of God. [14] The armies that were in heaven followed him on white horses, wearing pure white linen. [15] A sharp sword came from his mouth, so that he might strike the nations with it. He will rule them with an iron rod. He will also trample the winepress of the fierce anger of God, the Almighty. [16] And he has a name written on his robe and on his thigh: KING OF KINGS AND LORD OF LORDS.

Day 03

REFLECTION

What does Colossians 1:15–23 say Jesus has authority over?

QUESTIONS

Where in your life do you struggle to surrender to Jesus's authority?
What might it look like to turn those things over to Him?

THE NATURE OF THE KINGDOM

Day 04

God's kingdom is characterized by service, humility,
justice, righteousness, joy, and peace.

Isaiah 9:2–7

[2] The people walking in darkness
have seen a great light;
a light has dawned
on those living in the land of darkness.
[3] You have enlarged the nation
and increased its joy.
The people have rejoiced before you
as they rejoice at harvest time
and as they rejoice when dividing spoils.
[4] For you have shattered their oppressive yoke
and the rod on their shoulders,
the staff of their oppressor,
just as you did on the day of Midian.
[5] For every trampling boot of battle
and the bloodied garments of war
will be burned as fuel for the fire.
[6] For a child will be born for us,
a son will be given to us,
and the government will be on his shoulders.
He will be named
Wonderful Counselor, Mighty God,
Eternal Father, Prince of Peace.
[7] The dominion will be vast,
and its prosperity will never end.
He will reign on the throne of David
and over his kingdom,
to establish and sustain it
with justice and righteousness from now on and forever.
The zeal of the Lord of Armies will accomplish this.

Isaiah 61

MESSIAH'S JUBILEE

[1] The Spirit of the Lord God is on me,
because the Lord has anointed me
to bring good news to the poor.
He has sent me to heal the brokenhearted,
to proclaim liberty to the captives
and freedom to the prisoners;
[2] to proclaim the year of the Lord's favor,
and the day of our God's vengeance;
to comfort all who mourn,

³ to provide for those who mourn in Zion;
to give them a crown of beauty instead of ashes,
festive oil instead of mourning,
and splendid clothes instead of despair.
And they will be called righteous trees,
planted by the LORD
to glorify him.
⁴ They will rebuild the ancient ruins;
they will restore the former devastations;
they will renew the ruined cities,
the devastations of many generations.
⁵ Strangers will stand and feed your flocks,
and foreigners will be your plowmen and vinedressers.

⁶ But you will be called the LORD's priests;
they will speak of you as ministers of our God;
you will eat the wealth of the nations,
and you will boast in their riches.
⁷ In place of your shame, you will have a double portion;
in place of disgrace, they will rejoice over their share.
So they will possess double in their land,
and eternal joy will be theirs.

⁸ For I the LORD love justice;
I hate robbery and injustice;
I will faithfully reward my people
and make a permanent covenant with them.
⁹ Their descendants will be known among the nations,
and their posterity among the peoples.
All who see them will recognize
that they are a people the LORD has blessed.

¹⁰ I rejoice greatly in the LORD,
I exult in my God;
for he has clothed me with the garments of salvation
and wrapped me in a robe of righteousness,
as a groom wears a turban
and as a bride adorns herself with her jewels.
¹¹ For as the earth produces its growth,
and as a garden enables what is sown to spring up,
so the Lord GOD will cause righteousness and praise
to spring up before all the nations.

Matthew 4:12–25

MINISTRY IN GALILEE

[12] When he heard that John had been arrested, he withdrew into Galilee. [13] He left Nazareth and went to live in Capernaum by the sea, in the region of Zebulun and Naphtali. [14] This was to fulfill what was spoken through the prophet Isaiah:

[15] Land of Zebulun and land of Naphtali,
along the road by the sea, beyond the Jordan,
Galilee of the Gentiles.
[16] The people who live in darkness
have seen a great light,
and for those living in the land of the shadow of death,
a light has dawned.

[17] From then on Jesus began to preach, "Repent, because the kingdom of heaven has come near."

THE FIRST DISCIPLES

[18] As he was walking along the Sea of Galilee, he saw two brothers, Simon (who is called Peter), and his brother Andrew. They were casting a net into the sea—for they were fishermen. [19] "Follow me," he told them, "and I will make you fish for people." [20] Immediately they left their nets and followed him.

[21] Going on from there, he saw two other brothers, James the son of Zebedee, and his brother John. They were in a boat with Zebedee their father, preparing their nets, and he called them. [22] Immediately they left the boat and their father and followed him.

TEACHING, PREACHING, AND HEALING

[23] Now Jesus began to go all over Galilee, teaching in their synagogues, preaching the good news of the kingdom, and healing every disease and sickness among the people.

[24] Then the news about him spread throughout Syria. So they brought to him all those who were afflicted, those suffering from various diseases and intense pains, the demon-possessed, the epileptics, and the paralytics. And he healed them. [25] Large crowds followed him from Galilee, the Decapolis, Jerusalem, Judea, and beyond the Jordan.

Luke 4:16–21

REJECTION AT NAZARETH

[16] He came to Nazareth, where he had been brought up. As usual, he entered the synagogue on the Sabbath day and stood up to read. [17] The scroll of the prophet Isaiah was given to him, and unrolling the scroll, he found the place where it was written:

[18] The Spirit of the Lord is on me,
because he has anointed me
to preach good news to the poor.
He has sent me
to proclaim release to the captives
and recovery of sight to the blind,
to set free the oppressed,
[19] to proclaim the year of the Lord's favor.

[20] He then rolled up the scroll, gave it back to the attendant, and sat down. And the eyes of everyone in the synagogue were fixed on him. [21] He began by saying to them, "Today as you listen, this Scripture has been fulfilled."

Romans 14:13–19

[13] Therefore, let us no longer judge one another. Instead decide never to put a stumbling block or pitfall in the way of your brother or sister. [14] I know and am persuaded in the Lord Jesus that nothing is unclean in itself. Still, to someone who considers a thing to be unclean, to that one it is unclean. [15] For if your brother or sister is hurt by what you eat, you are no longer walking according to love. Do not destroy, by what you eat, someone for whom Christ died.

[16] Therefore, do not let your good be slandered, [17] for the kingdom of God is not eating and drinking, but righteousness, peace, and joy in the Holy Spirit.

[18] Whoever serves Christ in this way is acceptable to God and receives human approval.

[19] So then, let us pursue what promotes peace and what builds up one another.

Day 04

REFLECTION

How does the way of Jesus differ from the way of
the world? What about His way surprises you?

QUESTIONS

What is the "good news of the kingdom"
described in Matthew 4:23?

THE KINGDOM IS COMING

Having been inaugurated through Christ, God's already-active kingdom will be fully established when Jesus returns.

Isaiah 11:1–10

REIGN OF THE DAVIDIC KING

¹ Then a shoot will grow from the stump of Jesse,
and a branch from his roots will bear fruit.
² The Spirit of the LORD will rest on him—
a Spirit of wisdom and understanding,
a Spirit of counsel and strength,
a Spirit of knowledge and of the fear of the LORD.
³ His delight will be in the fear of the LORD.
He will not judge
by what he sees with his eyes,
he will not execute justice
by what he hears with his ears,
⁴ but he will judge the poor righteously
and execute justice for the oppressed of the land.
He will strike the land
with a scepter from his mouth,
and he will kill the wicked
with a command from his lips.
⁵ Righteousness will be a belt around his hips;
faithfulness will be a belt around his waist.

⁶ The wolf will dwell with the lamb,
and the leopard will lie down with the goat.
The calf, the young lion, and the fattened calf will be together,
and a child will lead them.
⁷ The cow and the bear will graze,
their young ones will lie down together,
and the lion will eat straw like cattle.
⁸ An infant will play beside the cobra's pit,
and a toddler will put his hand into a snake's den.
⁹ They will not harm or destroy each other
on my entire holy mountain,
for the land will be as full
of the knowledge of the LORD
as the sea is filled with water.

¹⁰ On that day the root of Jesse
will stand as a banner for the peoples.
The nations will look to him for guidance,
and his resting place will be glorious.

Luke 21:25–36

THE COMING OF THE SON OF MAN

²⁵ "Then there will be signs in the sun, moon, and stars; and there will be anguish on the earth among nations bewildered by the roaring of the sea and the waves. ²⁶ People will faint from fear and expectation of the things that are coming on the world, because the powers of the heavens will be shaken.

²⁷ Then they will see the Son of Man coming in a cloud with power and great glory.

²⁸ But when these things begin to take place, stand up and lift your heads, because your redemption is near."

THE PARABLE OF THE FIG TREE

²⁹ Then he told them a parable: "Look at the fig tree, and all the trees. ³⁰ As soon as they put out leaves you can see for yourselves and recognize that summer is already near. ³¹ In the same way, when you see these things happening, recognize that the kingdom of God is near. ³² Truly I tell you, this generation will certainly not pass away until all things take place. ³³ Heaven and earth will pass away, but my words will never pass away.

THE NEED FOR WATCHFULNESS

³⁴ "Be on your guard, so that your minds are not dulled from carousing, drunkenness, and worries of life, or that day will come on you unexpectedly ³⁵ like a trap. For it will come on all who live on the face of the whole earth. ³⁶ But be alert at all times, praying that you may have strength to escape all these things that are going to take place and to stand before the Son of Man."

Romans 8:18–25

FROM GROANS TO GLORY

¹⁸ For I consider that the sufferings of this present time are not worth comparing with the glory that is going to be revealed to us. ¹⁹ For the creation eagerly waits with anticipation for God's sons to be revealed. ²⁰ For the creation was subjected to futility—not willingly, but because of him who subjected it—in the hope ²¹ that the creation itself will also be set free from the bondage to decay into the

glorious freedom of God's children. ²² For we know that the whole creation has been groaning together with labor pains until now. ²³ Not only that, but we ourselves who have the Spirit as the firstfruits—we also groan within ourselves, eagerly waiting for adoption, the redemption of our bodies. ²⁴ Now in this hope we were saved, but hope that is seen is not hope, because who hopes for what he sees? ²⁵ Now if we hope for what we do not see, we eagerly wait for it with patience.

2 Timothy 2:8–13

⁸ Remember Jesus Christ, risen from the dead and descended from David, according to my gospel, ⁹ for which I suffer to the point of being bound like a criminal.

But the word of God is not bound.

¹⁰ This is why I endure all things for the elect: so that they also may obtain salvation, which is in Christ Jesus, with eternal glory. ¹¹ This saying is trustworthy:

> For if we died with him,
> we will also live with him;
> ¹² if we endure, we will also reign with him;
> if we deny him, he will also deny us;
> ¹³ if we are faithless, he remains faithful,
> for he cannot deny himself.

Day 05

REFLECTION

What are some visible and invisible signs that the
kingdom is already at work?

QUESTIONS

In light of Christ's return, how can you actively
participate in His kingdom today?

WHAT IS A PARABLE?

A parable is…

ALWAYS

A story with a purpose.

Told to initiate conversation
and prompt questions.

A memorable word picture,
easy to recall and retell.

Told to conceal truth from some
and reveal truth to others.

SOMETIMES

Told to address something
happening in the moment.

A story that uses symbolism.

Told to correct common misconceptions
and religious distortions.

Used to describe Jesus and
the kingdom of God.

NEVER

Intended for only one generation.

Told merely for entertainment.

Clearly understood by all who hear it.

Contrary to the rest of Scripture.

GRACE

Take this day to catch up on your reading, pray,
and rest in the presence of the Lord.

Day 06

DAY

Their descendants will be known among the nations,
and their posterity among the peoples.
All who see them will recognize
that they are a people the LORD has blessed.

Isaiah 61:9

WEEKLY

Scripture is God-breathed and true. When we memorize it, we
carry the good news of Jesus with us wherever we go.

As we read through Scripture about the kingdom of God, we will memorize the
Lord's Prayer together. This week we will memorize Matthew 6:9–10.

Day 07

TRUTH

"Our Father which art in heaven, Hallowed be thy name.
Thy kingdom come, Thy will be done in earth, as it is in heaven.
Give us this day our daily bread.
And forgive us our debts, as we forgive our debtors.
And lead us not into temptation, but deliver us from evil: For thine is
the kingdom, and the power, and the glory, for ever. Amen."

Matthew 6:9-13 KJV

LIFE IN THE KINGDOM OF GOD

Christ came as the perfect King and remains our perfect King today. He calls the Church to share in the building of His kingdom and to serve as a taste of the heavenly kingdom on earth.

In the Sermon on the Mount in Matthew 6–9, Jesus taught about how to live in anticipation of the coming kingdom that is with us now in part but will one day be realized in full. This sermon tells us what the kingdom of God is, what it is not, and how to live in light of the kingdom that is both now and yet to come.

Over the next two weeks, we will read what Scripture says about how to live as citizens of God's kingdom, here and now.

THE KING'S PEOPLE

Day 08

People from every nation will share in Jesus's kingdom inheritance and mission.

Hosea 2:23 NIV

"I will plant her for myself in the land;
  I will show my love to the one I called 'Not my
  loved one.'
I will say to those called 'Not my people,' 'You are
  my people';
  and they will say, 'You are my God.'"

Romans 8:12–17

THE HOLY SPIRIT'S MINISTRIES

12 So then, brothers and sisters, we are not obligated to the flesh to live according to the flesh, 13 because if you live according to the flesh, you are going to die. But if by the Spirit you put to death the deeds of the body, you will live. 14 For all those led by God's Spirit are God's sons. 15 For you did not receive a spirit of slavery to fall back into fear. Instead, you received the Spirit of adoption, by whom we cry out, "Abba, Father!" 16 The Spirit himself testifies together with our spirit that we are God's children, 17 and if children, also heirs—heirs of God and coheirs with Christ—if indeed we suffer with him so that we may also be glorified with him.

Ephesians 1:3–14

GOD'S RICH BLESSINGS

3 Blessed is the God and Father of our Lord Jesus Christ, who has blessed us with every spiritual blessing in the heavens in Christ. 4 For he chose us in him, before the foundation of the world, to be holy and blameless in love before him. 5 He predestined us to be adopted as sons through Jesus Christ for himself, according to the good pleasure of his will, 6 to the praise of his glorious grace that he lavished on us in the Beloved One.

[7] In him we have redemption through his blood, the forgiveness of our trespasses, according to the riches of his grace [8] that he richly poured out on us with all wisdom and understanding. [9] He made known to us the mystery of his will, according to his good pleasure that he purposed in Christ [10] as a plan for the right time—to bring everything together in Christ, both things in heaven and things on earth in him.

[11] In him we have also received an inheritance, because we were predestined according to the plan of the one who works out everything in agreement with the purpose of his will, [12] so that we who had already put our hope in Christ might bring praise to his glory.

[13] In him you also were sealed with the promised Holy Spirit when you heard the word of truth, the gospel of your salvation, and when you believed. [14] The Holy Spirit is the down payment of our inheritance, until the redemption of the possession, to the praise of his glory.

Ephesians 2:8–22

[8] For you are saved by grace through faith, and this is not from yourselves; it is God's gift— [9] not from works, so that no one can boast. [10] For we are his workmanship, created in Christ Jesus for good works, which God prepared ahead of time for us to do.

UNITY IN CHRIST

[11] So, then, remember that at one time you were Gentiles in the flesh—called "the uncircumcised" by those called "the circumcised," which is done in the flesh by human hands. [12] At that time you were without Christ, excluded from the citizenship of Israel, and foreigners to the covenants of promise, without hope and without God in the world. [13] But now in Christ Jesus, you who were far away have been brought near by the blood of Christ. [14] For he is our peace, who made both groups one and tore down the dividing wall of hostility. In his flesh, [15] he made of no effect the law consisting of commands and expressed in regulations, so that he might create in himself one new man from the two, resulting in peace. [16] He did this so that he might reconcile both to God in one body through the cross by which he put the hostility to death. [17] He came and proclaimed the good news of peace to you who were far away and peace to those who were near. [18] For through him we both have access in one Spirit to the Father. [19] So, then, you are no longer foreigners and strangers, but fellow citizens with the saints, and members of God's household, [20] built on the foundation of the apostles and prophets, with Christ Jesus himself as the cornerstone. [21] In him the whole building, being put together, grows into a holy temple in the Lord. [22] In him you are also being built together for God's dwelling in the Spirit.

Revelation 1:4–6

[4] John: To the seven churches in Asia. Grace and peace to you from the one who is, who was, and who is to come, and from the seven spirits before his throne, [5] and from Jesus Christ, the faithful witness, the firstborn from the dead and the ruler of the kings of the earth.

To him who loves us and has set us free from our sins by his blood, [6] and made us a kingdom, priests to his God and Father—to him be glory and dominion forever and ever. Amen.

Revelation 5:1–10

THE LAMB TAKES THE SCROLL

[1] Then I saw in the right hand of the one seated on the throne a scroll with writing on both sides, sealed with seven seals. [2] I also saw a mighty angel proclaiming with a loud voice, "Who is worthy to open the scroll and break its seals?" [3] But no one in heaven or on earth or under the earth was able to open the scroll or even to look in it. [4] I wept and wept because no one was found worthy to open the scroll or even to look in it. [5] Then one of the elders said to me, "Do not weep. Look, the Lion from the tribe of Judah, the Root of David, has conquered so that he is able to open the scroll and its seven seals."

[6] Then I saw one like a slaughtered lamb standing in the midst of the throne and the four living creatures and among the elders. He had seven horns and seven eyes, which are the seven spirits of God sent into all the earth. [7] He went and took the scroll out of the right hand of the one seated on the throne.

THE LAMB IS WORTHY

[8] When he took the scroll, the four living creatures and the twenty-four elders fell down before the Lamb. Each one had a harp and golden bowls filled with incense, which are the prayers of the saints. [9] And they sang a new song:

> You are worthy to take the scroll
> and to open its seals,
> because you were slaughtered,
> and you purchased people
> for God by your blood
> from every tribe and language
> and people and nation.
> [10] You made them a kingdom
> and priests to our God,
> and they will reign on the earth.

Day 08

REFLECTION

Read Romans 8:12–17 again. Who are God's
sons and daughters?

QUESTIONS

How has the blood of Christ paved the way
for unity among all believers?

THE KINGDOM IS THEIRS

The upside-down nature of the kingdom reframes our understanding of human struggles.

Day 09

Matthew 5:1–16

THE SERMON ON THE MOUNT

[1] When he saw the crowds, he went up on the mountain, and after he sat down, his disciples came to him. [2] Then he began to teach them, saying:

THE BEATITUDES

[3] "Blessed are the poor in spirit,
for the kingdom of heaven is theirs.
[4] Blessed are those who mourn,
for they will be comforted.
[5] Blessed are the humble,
for they will inherit the earth.
[6] Blessed are those who hunger and thirst for righteousness,
for they will be filled.
[7] Blessed are the merciful,
for they will be shown mercy.
[8] Blessed are the pure in heart,
for they will see God.
[9] Blessed are the peacemakers,
for they will be called sons of God.
[10] Blessed are those who are persecuted because of righteousness,
for the kingdom of heaven is theirs.

[11] "You are blessed when they insult you and persecute you and falsely say every kind of evil against you because of me. [12] Be glad and rejoice, because your reward is great in heaven. For that is how they persecuted the prophets who were before you.

BELIEVERS ARE SALT AND LIGHT

[13] "You are the salt of the earth. But if the salt should lose its taste, how can it be made salty? It's no longer good for anything but to be thrown out and trampled under people's feet.

[14] "You are the light of the world. A city situated on a hill cannot be hidden. [15] No one lights a lamp and puts it under a basket, but rather

on a lampstand, and it gives light for all who are in the house. [16] In the same way, let your light shine before others, so that they may see your good works and give glory to your Father in heaven."

Psalm 69:29–33

[29] But as for me—poor and in pain—
let your salvation protect me, God.
[30] I will praise God's name with song
and exalt him with thanksgiving.
[31] That will please the LORD more than an ox,
more than a bull with horns and hooves.
[32] The humble will see it and rejoice.
You who seek God, take heart!
[33] For the LORD listens to the needy
and does not despise
his own who are prisoners.

Isaiah 49:6

He says,
"It is not enough for you to be my servant
raising up the tribes of Jacob
and restoring the protected ones of Israel.
I will also make you a light for the nations,
to be my salvation to the ends of the earth."

Mark 10:32–45

THE THIRD PREDICTION OF HIS DEATH

[32] They were on the road, going up to Jerusalem, and Jesus was walking ahead of them. The disciples were astonished, but those who followed him were afraid. Taking the Twelve aside again, he began to tell them the things that would happen to him. [33] "See, we are going up to Jerusalem. The Son of Man will be handed over to the chief priests and the scribes, and they will condemn him to death. Then they will hand him over to the Gentiles, [34] and they will mock him, spit on him, flog him, and kill him, and he will rise after three days."

SUFFERING AND SERVICE

[35] James and John, the sons of Zebedee, approached him and said, "Teacher, we want you to do whatever we ask you."

[36] "What do you want me to do for you?" he asked them.

[37] They answered him, "Allow us to sit at your right and at your left in your glory."

[38] Jesus said to them, "You don't know what you're asking. Are you able to drink the cup I drink or to be baptized with the baptism I am baptized with?"

[39] "We are able," they told him.

Jesus said to them, "You will drink the cup I drink, and you will be baptized with the baptism I am baptized with. [40] But to sit at my right or left is not mine to give; instead, it is for those for whom it has been prepared."

[41] When the ten disciples heard this, they began to be indignant with James and John. [42] Jesus called them over and said to them, "You know that those who are regarded as rulers of the Gentiles lord it over them, and those in high positions act as tyrants over them. [43] But it is not so among you.

On the contrary, whoever wants to become great among you will be your servant, [44] and whoever wants to be first among you will be a slave to all.

[45] For even the Son of Man did not come to be served, but to serve, and to give his life as a ransom for many."

Colossians 4:2–6

SPEAKING TO GOD AND OTHERS

[2] Devote yourselves to prayer; stay alert in it with thanksgiving. [3] At the same time, pray also for us that God may open a door to us for the word, to speak the mystery of Christ, for which I am in chains, [4] so that I may make it known as I should. [5] Act wisely toward outsiders, making the most of the time. [6] Let your speech always be gracious, seasoned with salt, so that you may know how you should answer each person.

Day 09

REFLECTION

In what ways has Christ embodied these beatitudes through His life, death, and resurrection? What are some specific ways you can imitate Him?

QUESTIONS

Where is God calling you to be salt and light in the world today, as an ambassador of His kingdom?

THE LAW OF THE KINGDOM

Day 10

Our relationship to the Old Testament law is changed in Jesus, who fulfills the law and clarifies the ethics that characterize the kingdom.

Matthew 5:17–48

CHRIST FULFILLS THE LAW

17 "Don't think that I came to abolish the Law or the Prophets. I did not come to abolish but to fulfill. 18 For truly I tell you, until heaven and earth pass away, not the smallest letter or one stroke of a letter will pass away from the law until all things are accomplished. 19 Therefore, whoever breaks one of the least of these commands and teaches others to do the same will be called least in the kingdom of heaven. But whoever does and teaches these commands will be called great in the kingdom of heaven. 20 For I tell you, unless your righteousness surpasses that of the scribes and Pharisees, you will never get into the kingdom of heaven.

MURDER BEGINS IN THE HEART

21 "You have heard that it was said to our ancestors, Do not murder, and whoever murders will be subject to judgment. 22 But I tell you, everyone who is angry with his brother or sister will be subject to judgment. Whoever insults his brother or sister, will be subject to the court. Whoever says, 'You fool!' will be subject to hellfire. 23 So if you are offering your gift on the altar, and there you remember that your brother or sister has something against you, 24 leave your gift there in front of the altar. First go and be reconciled with your brother or sister, and then come and offer your gift. 25 Reach a settlement quickly with your adversary while you're on the way with him to the court, or your adversary will hand you over to the judge, and the judge to the officer, and you will be thrown into prison. 26 Truly I tell you, you will never get out of there until you have paid the last penny.

ADULTERY BEGINS IN THE HEART

[27] "You have heard that it was said, Do not commit adultery. [28] But I tell you, everyone who looks at a woman lustfully has already committed adultery with her in his heart. [29] If your right eye causes you to sin, gouge it out and throw it away. For it is better that you lose one of the parts of your body than for your whole body to be thrown into hell. [30] And if your right hand causes you to sin, cut it off and throw it away. For it is better that you lose one of the parts of your body than for your whole body to go into hell.

DIVORCE PRACTICES CENSURED

[31] "It was also said, Whoever divorces his wife must give her a written notice of divorce. [32] But I tell you, everyone who divorces his wife, except in a case of sexual immorality, causes her to commit adultery. And whoever marries a divorced woman commits adultery.

TELL THE TRUTH

[33] "Again, you have heard that it was said to our ancestors, You must not break your oath, but you must keep your oaths to the Lord. [34] But I tell you, don't take an oath at all: either by heaven, because it is God's throne; [35] or by the earth, because it is his footstool; or by Jerusalem, because it is the city of the great King. [36] Do not swear by your head, because you cannot make a single hair white or black. [37] But let your 'yes' mean 'yes,' and your 'no' mean 'no.' Anything more than this is from the evil one.

GO THE SECOND MILE

[38] "You have heard that it was said, An eye for an eye and a tooth for a tooth. [39] But I tell you, don't resist an evildoer. On the contrary, if anyone slaps you on your right cheek, turn the other to him also. [40] As for the one who wants to sue you and take away your shirt, let him have your coat as well. [41] And if anyone forces you to go one mile, go with him two. [42] Give to the one who asks you, and don't turn away from the one who wants to borrow from you.

LOVE YOUR ENEMIES

[43] "You have heard that it was said, Love your neighbor and hate your enemy. [44] But I tell you, love your enemies and pray for those who persecute you, [45] so that you may be children of your Father in heaven. For he causes his sun to rise on the evil and the good, and sends rain on the righteous and the unrighteous. [46] For if you love those who love you, what reward will you have? Don't even the tax collectors do the same? [47] And if you greet only your brothers and sisters, what are you doing out of the ordinary? Don't even the Gentiles do the same? [48] Be perfect, therefore, as your heavenly Father is perfect."

Matthew 13:47–52

THE PARABLE OF THE NET

47 "Again, the kingdom of heaven is like a large net thrown into the sea. It collected every kind of fish, 48 and when it was full, they dragged it ashore, sat down, and gathered the good fish into containers, but threw out the worthless ones. 49 So it will be at the end of the age. The angels will go out, separate the evil people from the righteous, 50 and throw them into the blazing furnace, where there will be weeping and gnashing of teeth.

THE STOREHOUSE OF TRUTH

51 "Have you understood all these things?"

They answered him, "Yes."

52 "Therefore," he said to them, "every teacher of the law who has become a disciple in the kingdom of heaven is like the owner of a house who brings out of his storeroom treasures new and old."

Psalm 40:6–8

6 You do not delight in sacrifice and offering;
you open my ears to listen.
You do not ask for a whole burnt offering or a sin offering.
7 Then I said, "See, I have come;
in the scroll it is written about me.
8 I delight to do your will, my God,
and your instruction is deep within me."

Hosea 6:6

For I desire faithful love and not sacrifice,
the knowledge of God rather than burnt offerings.

Micah 6:8

Mankind, he has told each of you what is good
and what it is the LORD requires of you:
to act justly,
to love faithfulness,
and to walk humbly with your God.

Mark 12:28–34

THE PRIMARY COMMANDS

28 One of the scribes approached. When he heard them debating and saw that Jesus answered them well, he asked him, "Which command is the most important of all?"

29 Jesus answered, "The most important is Listen, Israel! The Lord our God, the Lord is one. 30 Love the Lord your God with all your heart, with all your soul, with all your mind, and with all your strength. 31 The second is, Love your neighbor as yourself. There is no other command greater than these."

32 Then the scribe said to him, "You are right, teacher. You have correctly said that he is one, and there is no one else except him. 33 And to love him with all your heart, with all your understanding, and with all your strength, and to love your neighbor as yourself, is far more important than all the burnt offerings and sacrifices."

34 When Jesus saw that he answered wisely, he said to him, "You are not far from the kingdom of God." And no one dared to question him any longer.

Day 10

REFLECTION

How does the Spirit equip you to understand and
obey Jesus's instructions?

QUESTIONS

How does Mark 12:28–34 frame your
understanding of the law?

Jesus Interprets the Law

The Sermon on the Mount has been called Jesus's commentary on the Ten Commandments because it is Jesus's exposition of the law in the four Gospels. In it, He contrasts the law as interpreted by the Pharisees with the true nature and character of God's law.

The following excerpts from the Sermon on the Mount, known among scholars as the "Six Antitheses," follow the pattern, "You have heard that it was said...but I tell you..." In these passages, Jesus examines the intentions of the heart, deepening our understanding of God's law.

Ex 20:13
Dt 5:17

Murder

Mt 5:21-22

"You have heard that it was said…"

"Do not murder, and whoever murders will be subject to judgment."

Jesus used this widely-accepted command to address superficial attitudes and interpretations of God's law.

"But I tell you…"

"…everyone who is angry with his brother or sister will be subject to judgment. Whoever insults his brother or sister, will be subject to the court."

A violent temper, or the defiling of another's reputation, reflects a murderous heart.

Ex 20:14
Dt 5:18

Adultery

Mt 5:27-28

"You have heard that it was said…"

"Do not commit adultery."

Many considered adulterous actions to be the only form of infidelity and regarded indulging adulterous desires as a lesser transgression.

"But I tell you…"

"…everyone who looks at a woman lustfully has already committed adultery with her in his heart."

As with murder, infidelity begins in the heart.

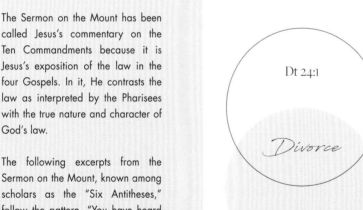

Dt 24:1

Divorce

Mt 5:31-32

"It was also said…"

"Whoever divorces his wife must give her a written notice of divorce."

Rabbinical interpretations of Deuteronomy 24:1 had become lax over the centuries, permitting a man to divorce his wife for such frivolous reasons as burning a meal or losing her physical beauty.

"But I tell you…"

"…everyone who divorces his wife, except in a case of sexual immorality, causes her to commit adultery. And whoever marries a divorced woman commits adultery."

Marriage is a relationship built on a covenant promise to love and cherish until death separates the husband and wife. This covenant should not be entered into, or dissolved, lightly.

Lv 19:12
Nm 30:2
Dt 23:21

Oaths

Mt 5:33, 37

"You have heard that it was said…"

"You must not break your oath, but you must keep your oaths to the Lord."

Oaths were binding, especially those taken in God's name. To break an oath taken in His name publicly dishonored His reputation.

"But I tell you…"

"…let your 'yes' mean 'yes,' and your 'no' mean 'no.' Anything more than this is from the evil one."

Our promises should stand as matters of personal integrity without having to invoke the name of the Lord.

Ex 21:14
Lv 24:20
Dt 19:21

Revenge

Mt 5:38-39

"You have heard that it was said…"

"An eye for an eye and a tooth for a tooth."

This instruction was given to help reach fair settlements in court, not as a prescription for personal retaliation.

"But I tell you…"

"…don't resist an evildoer. On the contrary, if anyone slaps you on your right cheek, turn the other to him also."

Here Jesus calls insult and brutality evil, but also instructs us to yield our right to vengeance to God.

Lv 19:18

Love for Enemies

Mt 5:43-44

"You have heard that it was said…"

"Love your neighbor and hate your enemy."

The command to hate your enemies does not appear anywhere in the Old Testament. Some teachers of the law believed the call to love our neighbors implied that we are free to do the opposite with our enemies.

"But I tell you…"

"…love your enemies and pray for those who persecute you…"

Love is the guiding principle for the Christian life, and prayer is an expression of this love.

Generosity, prayer, and fasting can focus
our motivations and actions on God's will
and His kingdom.

GOD'S KINGDOM COME

Matthew 6:1–18

HOW TO GIVE

[1] "Be careful not to practice your righteousness in front of others to be seen by them. Otherwise, you have no reward with your Father in heaven. [2] So whenever you give to the poor, don't sound a trumpet before you, as the hypocrites do in the synagogues and on the streets, to be applauded by people. Truly I tell you, they have their reward. [3] But when you give to the poor, don't let your left hand know what your right hand is doing, [4] so that your giving may be in secret. And your Father who sees in secret will reward you.

HOW TO PRAY

[5] "Whenever you pray, you must not be like the hypocrites, because they love to pray standing in the synagogues and on the street corners to be seen by people. Truly I tell you, they have their reward. [6] But when you pray, go into your private room, shut your door, and pray to your Father who is in secret. And your Father who sees in secret will reward you. [7] When you pray, don't babble like the Gentiles, since they imagine they'll be heard for their many words. [8] Don't be like them, because your Father knows the things you need before you ask him.

THE LORD'S PRAYER

[9] "Therefore, you should pray like this:

> Our Father in heaven,
> your name be honored as holy.
> [10] Your kingdom come.
> Your will be done
> on earth as it is in heaven.
> [11] Give us today our daily bread.
> [12] And forgive us our debts,
> as we also have forgiven our debtors.
> [13] And do not bring us into temptation,
> but deliver us from the evil one.

[14] "For if you forgive others their offenses, your heavenly Father will forgive you as well. [15] But if you don't forgive others, your Father will not forgive your offenses.

HOW TO FAST

[16] "Whenever you fast, don't be gloomy like the hypocrites. For they disfigure their faces so that their fasting is obvious to people. Truly I tell you, they have their reward. [17] But when you fast, put oil on your head and wash your face, [18] so that your fasting isn't obvious to others but to your Father who is in secret. And your Father who sees in secret will reward you."

Matthew 26:36–46

[36] Then Jesus came with them to a place called Gethsemane, and he told the disciples, "Sit here while I go over there and pray." [37] Taking along Peter and the two sons of Zebedee, he began to be sorrowful and troubled. [38] He said to them, "I am deeply grieved to the point of death. Remain here and stay awake with me." [39] Going a little farther, he fell facedown and prayed, "My Father, if it is possible, let this cup pass from me. Yet not as I will, but as you will."

[40] Then he came to the disciples and found them sleeping. He asked Peter, "So, couldn't you stay awake with me one hour? [41] Stay awake and pray, so that you won't enter into temptation. The spirit is willing, but the flesh is weak."

[42] Again, a second time, he went away and prayed, "My Father, if this cannot pass unless I drink it, your will be done." [43] And he came again and found them sleeping, because they could not keep their eyes open.

[44] After leaving them, he went away again and prayed a third time, saying the same thing once more. [45] Then he came to the disciples and said to them, "Are you still sleeping and resting? See, the time is near. The Son of Man is betrayed into the hands of sinners. [46] Get up; let's go. See, my betrayer is near."

Luke 18:9–14

THE PARABLE OF THE PHARISEE AND THE TAX COLLECTOR

[9] He also told this parable to some who trusted in themselves that they were righteous and looked down on everyone else: [10] "Two men went up to the temple to pray, one a Pharisee and the other a tax collector. [11] The Pharisee was standing and praying like this about himself: 'God, I thank you that I'm not like other people—greedy, unrighteous, adulterers, or even like this tax collector. [12] I fast twice a week; I give a tenth of everything I get.'

[13] "But the tax collector, standing far off, would not even raise his eyes to heaven but kept striking his chest and saying, 'God, have mercy on me, a sinner!' [14] I tell you, this one went down to his house justified rather than the other, because everyone who exalts himself will be humbled, but the one who humbles himself will be exalted."

Day 11

REFLECTION

What do Jesus's instructions for practicing these different spiritual disciplines have in common?

QUESTIONS

Where do you find yourself trying to give the impression of
godliness, rather than actually pursuing God?

THE
KINGDOM
OF THIS
WORLD IS
BECOME THE

KINGDOM OF OUR LORD, AND OF HIS CHRIST

Handel's *Messiah*: "Hallelujah Chorus"

TREASURES OF THE KINGDOM

Day 12

Our priority is to seek the kingdom over earthly possessions,
replacing worry with trust in God's provision.

Matthew 6:19–34

GOD AND POSSESSIONS

[19] "Don't store up for yourselves treasures on earth, where moth and rust destroy and where thieves break in and steal. [20] But store up for yourselves treasures in heaven, where neither moth nor rust destroys, and where thieves don't break in and steal. [21] For where your treasure is, there your heart will be also.

[22] "The eye is the lamp of the body. If your eye is healthy, your whole body will be full of light. [23] But if your eye is bad, your whole body will be full of darkness. So if the light within you is darkness, how deep is that darkness!

[24] "No one can serve two masters, since either he will hate one and love the other, or he will be devoted to one and despise the other. You cannot serve both God and money.

[25] "Therefore I tell you: Don't worry about your life, what you will eat or what you will drink; or about your body, what you will wear. Isn't life more than food and the body more than clothing? [26] Consider the birds of the sky: They don't sow or reap or gather into barns, yet your heavenly Father feeds them. Aren't you worth more than they? [27] Can any of you add one moment to his life span by worrying? [28] And why do you worry about clothes? Observe how the wildflowers of the field grow: They don't labor or spin thread. [29] Yet I tell you that not even Solomon in all his splendor was adorned like one of these. [30] If that's how God clothes the grass of the field, which is here today and thrown into the furnace tomorrow, won't he do much more for you—you of little faith? [31] So don't worry, saying, 'What will we eat?' or 'What will we drink?' or 'What will we wear?' [32] For the Gentiles eagerly seek all these things, and your heavenly Father knows that you need them.

[33] But seek first the kingdom of God and his righteousness, and all these things will be provided for you.

[34] Therefore don't worry about tomorrow, because tomorrow will worry about itself. Each day has enough trouble of its own."

Matthew 7:1–6

[1] "Do not judge, so that you won't be judged. [2] For you will be judged by the same standard with which you judge others, and you will be measured by the same measure you use. [3] Why do you look at the splinter in your brother's eye but don't notice the beam of wood in your own eye? [4] Or how can you say to your brother, 'Let me take the splinter out of your eye,' and look, there's a beam of wood in your own eye? [5] Hypocrite! First take the beam of wood out of your eye, and then you

will see clearly to take the splinter out of your brother's eye. ⁶ Don't give what is holy to dogs or toss your pearls before pigs, or they will trample them under their feet, turn, and tear you to pieces."

Matthew 13:44–45

THE PARABLES OF THE HIDDEN TREASURE AND OF THE PRICELESS PEARL

⁴⁴ "The kingdom of heaven is like treasure, buried in a field, that a man found and reburied. Then in his joy he goes and sells everything he has and buys that field.

⁴⁵ "Again, the kingdom of heaven is like a merchant in search of fine pearls. ⁴⁶ When he found one priceless pearl, he went and sold everything he had and bought it."

Psalm 147:7–11

⁷ Sing to the Lord with thanksgiving;
play the lyre to our God,
⁸ who covers the sky with clouds,
prepares rain for the earth,
and causes grass to grow on the hills.
⁹ He provides the animals with their food,
and the young ravens what they cry for.

¹⁰ He is not impressed by the strength of a horse;
he does not value the power of a warrior.
¹¹ The Lord values those who fear him,
those who put their hope in his faithful love.

Luke 12:32–34

³² "Don't be afraid, little flock, because your Father delights to give you the kingdom. ³³ Sell your possessions and give to the poor. Make money-bags for yourselves that won't grow old, an inexhaustible treasure in heaven, where no thief comes near and no moth destroys. ³⁴ For where your treasure is, there your heart will be also."

Day 12

REFLECTION

Thinking about Jesus's teaching in today's reading,
what things are valuable in the kingdom?

QUESTIONS

What specific things do you worry about most? What promises and instructions does Jesus give in Matthew 6:25–34 to address these anxieties?

GRACE

Take this day to catch up on your reading, pray,
and rest in the presence of the Lord.

Day 13

DAY

To him who loves us and has set us free from our sins by his blood, and made us a kingdom, priests to his God and Father—to him be glory and dominion forever and ever. Amen.

Revelation 1:5-6

WEEKLY

Scripture is God-breathed and true. When we memorize it, we
carry the good news of Jesus with us wherever we go.

As we read through Scripture about the kingdom of God, we will memorize
the Lord's Prayer together. The second part of the prayer reminds us to trust
God to meet our needs, and to extend forgiveness to others because we are
a forgiven people.

Day 14

TRUTH

"Our Father which art in heaven, Hallowed be thy name.
Thy kingdom come, Thy will be done in earth, as it is in heaven.
Give us this day our daily bread.
And forgive us our debts, as we forgive our debtors.
And lead us not into temptation, but deliver us from evil: For thine is
the kingdom, and the power, and the glory, for ever. Amen."

Matthew 6:9-13 KJV

ENTERING THE KINGDOM

THE KINGDOM OF GOD

Matthew 7:7–29

ASK, SEARCH, KNOCK

[7] "Ask, and it will be given to you. Seek, and you will find. Knock, and the door will be opened to you. [8] For everyone who asks receives, and the one who seeks finds, and to the one who knocks, the door will be opened. [9] Who among you, if his son asks him for bread, will give him a stone? [10] Or if he asks for a fish, will give him a snake? [11] If you then, who are evil, know how to give good gifts to your children, how much more will your Father in heaven give good things to those who ask him. [12] Therefore, whatever you want others to do for you, do also the same for them, for this is the Law and the Prophets.

ENTERING THE KINGDOM

[13] "Enter through the narrow gate. For the gate is wide and the road broad that leads to destruction, and there are many who go through it. [14] How narrow is the gate and difficult the road that leads to life, and few find it.

[15] "Be on your guard against false prophets who come to you in sheep's clothing but inwardly are ravaging wolves. [16] You'll recognize them by their fruit. Are grapes gathered from thornbushes or figs from thistles? [17] In the same way, every good tree produces good fruit, but a bad tree produces bad fruit. [18] A good tree can't produce bad fruit; neither can a bad tree produce good fruit. [19] Every tree that doesn't produce good fruit is cut down and thrown into the fire. [20] So you'll recognize them by their fruit.

[21] "Not everyone who says to me, 'Lord, Lord,' will enter the kingdom of heaven, but only the one who does the will of my Father in heaven. [22] On that day many will say to me, 'Lord, Lord, didn't we prophesy in your name, drive out demons in your name, and do many miracles in your name?' [23] Then I will announce to them, 'I never knew you. Depart from me, you lawbreakers!'

THE TWO FOUNDATIONS

[24] "Therefore, everyone who hears these words of mine and acts on them will be like a wise man who built his house on the rock. [25] The rain fell, the rivers rose, and the winds blew and pounded that house. Yet it didn't

collapse, because its foundation was on the rock. [26] But everyone who hears these words of mine and doesn't act on them will be like a foolish man who built his house on the sand. [27] The rain fell, the rivers rose, the winds blew and pounded that house, and it collapsed. It collapsed with a great crash."

[28] When Jesus had finished saying these things, the crowds were astonished at his teaching, [29] because he was teaching them like one who had authority, and not like their scribes.

Psalm 16:7–11

[7] I will bless the LORD who counsels me—
even at night when my thoughts trouble me.
[8] I always let the LORD guide me.
Because he is at my right hand,
I will not be shaken.

[9] Therefore my heart is glad
and my whole being rejoices;
my body also rests securely.
[10] For you will not abandon me to Sheol;
you will not allow your faithful one to see decay.
[11] You reveal the path of life to me;
in your presence is abundant joy;
at your right hand are eternal pleasures.

Matthew 13:24–30, 36–43

THE PARABLE OF THE WHEAT AND THE WEEDS

[24] He presented another parable to them: "The kingdom of heaven may be compared to a man who sowed good seed in his field. [25] But while people were sleeping, his enemy came, sowed weeds among the wheat, and left. [26] When the plants sprouted and produced grain, then the weeds also appeared. [27] The landowner's servants came to him and said, 'Master, didn't you sow good seed in your field? Then where did the weeds come from?'

[28] "'An enemy did this,' he told them.

"'So, do you want us to go and pull them up?' the servants asked him.

[29] "'No,' he said. 'When you pull up the weeds, you might also uproot the wheat with them. [30] Let both grow together until the harvest. At harvest time I'll tell the reapers: Gather the weeds first and tie them in bundles to burn them, but collect the wheat in my barn.'"

…

[36] Then he left the crowds and went into the house. His disciples approached him and said, "Explain to us the parable of the weeds in the field."

[37] He replied, "The one who sows the good seed is the Son of Man; [38] the field is the world; and the good seed—these are the children of the kingdom. The weeds are the children of the evil one, [39] and the enemy who sowed them is the devil. The harvest is the end of the age, and the harvesters are angels. [40] Therefore, just as the weeds are gathered and burned in the fire, so it will be at the end of the age. [41] The Son of Man will send out his angels, and they will gather from his kingdom all who cause sin and those guilty of lawlessness. [42] They will throw them into the blazing furnace where there will be weeping and gnashing of teeth. [43] Then the righteous will shine like the sun in their Father's kingdom. Let anyone who has ears listen."

Matthew 22:1–14

THE PARABLE OF THE WEDDING BANQUET

[1] Once more Jesus spoke to them in parables: [2] "The kingdom of heaven is like a king who gave a wedding banquet for his son. [3] He sent his servants to summon those invited to the banquet, but they didn't want to come. [4] Again, he sent out other servants and said, 'Tell those who are invited: See, I've prepared my dinner; my oxen and fattened cattle have been slaughtered, and everything is ready. Come to the wedding banquet.'

[5] "But they paid no attention and went away, one to his own farm, another to his business, [6] while the rest seized his servants, mistreated them, and killed them. [7] The king was enraged, and he sent out his troops, killed those murderers, and burned down their city.

[8] "Then he told his servants, 'The banquet is ready, but those who were invited were not worthy. [9] Go then to where the roads exit the city and invite everyone you find to the banquet.' [10] So those servants went out on the roads and gathered everyone they found, both evil and good. The wedding banquet was filled with guests. [11] When the king came in to see the guests, he saw a man there who was not dressed for a wedding. [12] So he said to him, 'Friend, how did you get in here without wedding clothes?' The man was speechless.

[13] "Then the king told the attendants, 'Tie him up hand and foot, and throw him into the outer darkness, where there will be weeping and gnashing of teeth.'

[14] "For many are invited, but few are chosen."

Day 15

REFLECTION

In your own words, describe Jesus's warning about
who will and who will not enter the kingdom.

QUESTIONS

In the parable of the wedding banquet, why did Jesus say that "many are invited, but few are chosen" (Matthew 22:14)? Where do you see this happening today?

ANTICIPATING THE KINGDOM

Day 16

While we wait for Christ's return, the Spirit equips us
to live faithfully in light of our redemption in Christ.

Matthew 25:1–13

THE PARABLE OF THE TEN VIRGINS

¹ "At that time the kingdom of heaven will be like ten virgins who took their lamps and went out to meet the groom. ² Five of them were foolish and five were wise. ³ When the foolish took their lamps, they didn't take oil with them; ⁴ but the wise ones took oil in their flasks with their lamps. ⁵ When the groom was delayed, they all became drowsy and fell asleep.

⁶ "In the middle of the night there was a shout: 'Here's the groom! Come out to meet him.'

⁷ "Then all the virgins got up and trimmed their lamps. ⁸ The foolish ones said to the wise ones, 'Give us some of your oil, because our lamps are going out.'

⁹ "The wise ones answered, 'No, there won't be enough for us and for you. Go instead to those who sell oil, and buy some for yourselves.'

¹⁰ "When they had gone to buy some, the groom arrived, and those who were ready went in with him to the wedding banquet, and the door was shut. ¹¹ Later the rest of the virgins also came and said, 'Master, master, open up for us!'

¹² "He replied, 'Truly I tell you, I don't know you!'

¹³ "Therefore be alert, because you don't know either the day or the hour."

John 14:1–4, 18, 25–26

[1] "Don't let your heart be troubled. Believe in God; believe also in me. [2] In my Father's house are many rooms. If it were not so, would I have told you that I am going to prepare a place for you? [3] If I go away and prepare a place for you, I will come again and take you to myself, so that where I am you may be also. [4] You know the way to where I am going."

...

[18] "I will not leave you as orphans; I am coming to you."

...

[25] "I have spoken these things to you while I remain with you. [26] But the Counselor, the Holy Spirit, whom the Father will send in my name, will teach you all things and remind you of everything I have told you."

Colossians 3:1–17

THE LIFE OF THE NEW MAN

[1] So if you have been raised with Christ, seek the things above, where Christ is, seated at the right hand of God. [2] Set your minds on things above, not on earthly things. [3] For you died, and your life is hidden with Christ in God. [4] When Christ, who is your life, appears, then you also will appear with him in glory.

[5] Therefore, put to death what belongs to your earthly nature: sexual immorality, impurity, lust, evil desire, and greed, which is idolatry. [6] Because of these, God's wrath is coming upon the disobedient, [7] and you once walked in these things when you were living in them. [8] But now, put away all the following: anger, wrath, malice, slander, and filthy language from your mouth. [9] Do not lie to one another, since you have put off the old self with its practices [10] and have put on the new self. You are being renewed in knowledge according to the image of your Creator. [11] In Christ there is not Greek and Jew, circumcision and uncircumcision, barbarian, Scythian, slave and free; but Christ is all and in all.

THE CHRISTIAN LIFE

[12] Therefore, as God's chosen ones, holy and dearly loved, put on compassion, kindness, humility, gentleness, and patience, [13] bearing with one another and forgiving one another if anyone has a grievance against another. Just as the Lord has forgiven you, so you are also to forgive. [14] Above all, put on love, which is the perfect bond of unity. [15] And let the peace of Christ, to which you were also called in one body, rule your hearts. And be thankful. [16] Let the word of Christ dwell richly among you, in all wisdom teaching and admonishing one another through

psalms, hymns, and spiritual songs, singing to God with gratitude in your hearts. [17] And whatever you do, in word or in deed, do everything in the name of the Lord Jesus, giving thanks to God the Father through him.

Romans 8:28–30

[28] We know that all things work together for the good of those who love God, who are called according to his purpose. [29] For those he foreknew he also predestined to be conformed to the image of his Son, so that he would be the firstborn among many brothers and sisters. [30] And those he predestined, he also called; and those he called, he also justified; and those he justified, he also glorified.

2 Peter 3:11–14

[11] Since all these things are to be dissolved in this way, it is clear what sort of people you should be in holy conduct and godliness [12] as you wait for the day of God and hasten its coming. Because of that day, the heavens will be dissolved with fire and the elements will melt with heat.

[13] But based on his promise, we wait for new heavens and a new earth, where righteousness dwells.

[14] Therefore, dear friends, while you wait for these things, make every effort to be found without spot or blemish in his sight, at peace.

Day 16

REFLECTION

How does John 14:1–4 motivate you to live faithfully
as you wait for Christ's return?

QUESTIONS

What is one "earthly thing" that preoccupies your mind? Which "things above" are helpful to remember in response (Colossians 3:2)?

THE KINGDOM OF GOD IN THE OLD TESTAMENT

From the Pentateuch to the Prophets, Scripture builds anticipation for Jesus—the One who will inaugurate the kingdom of God on earth with His first coming and bring the kingdom to its fullness with His return. Although the phrase "kingdom of God" does not appear in the Old Testament, the concept is evident throughout.

The following pages feature an overview of what the Old Testament says about the kingdom of God.

God is the sovereign King over all.

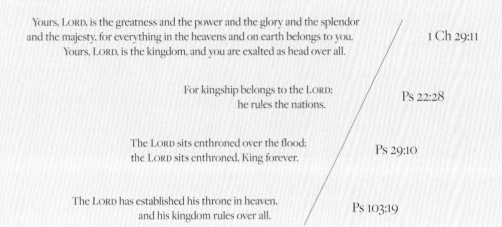

Yours, LORD, is the greatness and the power and the glory and the splendor and the majesty, for everything in the heavens and on earth belongs to you. Yours, LORD, is the kingdom, and you are exalted as head over all.

1 Ch 29:11

For kingship belongs to the LORD; he rules the nations.

Ps 22:28

The LORD sits enthroned over the flood; the LORD sits enthroned, King forever.

Ps 29:10

The LORD has established his throne in heaven, and his kingdom rules over all.

Ps 103:19

His kingdom is an everlasting kingdom.

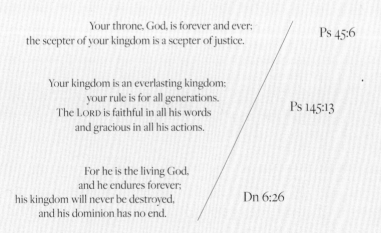

Your throne, God, is forever and ever; the scepter of your kingdom is a scepter of justice.

Ps 45:6

Your kingdom is an everlasting kingdom; your rule is for all generations. The LORD is faithful in all his words and gracious in all his actions.

Ps 145:13

For he is the living God, and he endures forever; his kingdom will never be destroyed, and his dominion has no end.

Dn 6:26

A promised Messiah will bring the kingdom and rule with humility, justice, righteousness, joy, and peace.

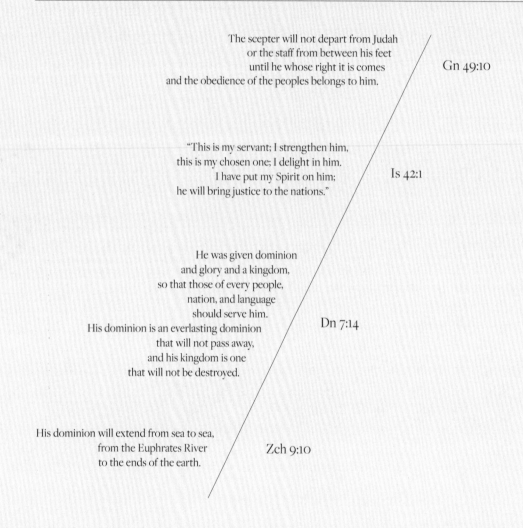

The scepter will not depart from Judah
or the staff from between his feet
until he whose right it is comes
and the obedience of the peoples belongs to him.

Gn 49:10

"This is my servant; I strengthen him,
this is my chosen one; I delight in him.
I have put my Spirit on him;
he will bring justice to the nations."

Is 42:1

He was given dominion
and glory and a kingdom,
so that those of every people,
nation, and language
should serve him.
His dominion is an everlasting dominion
that will not pass away,
and his kingdom is one
that will not be destroyed.

Dn 7:14

His dominion will extend from sea to sea,
from the Euphrates River
to the ends of the earth.

Zch 9:10

The people of God will inherit the kingdom and possess it forever.

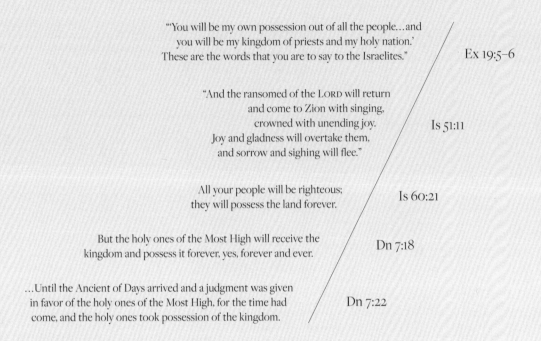

"'You will be my own possession out of all the people…and you will be my kingdom of priests and my holy nation.' These are the words that you are to say to the Israelites."

Ex 19:5–6

"And the ransomed of the LORD will return and come to Zion with singing, crowned with unending joy. Joy and gladness will overtake them, and sorrow and sighing will flee."

Is 51:11

All your people will be righteous; they will possess the land forever.

Is 60:21

But the holy ones of the Most High will receive the kingdom and possess it forever, yes, forever and ever.

Dn 7:18

…Until the Ancient of Days arrived and a judgment was given in favor of the holy ones of the Most High, for the time had come, and the holy ones took possession of the kingdom.

Dn 7:22

The kingdom, in its fullness, is a spiritual and physical realm in which the heavens and earth are recreated.

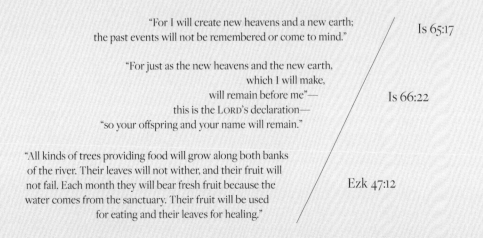

"For I will create new heavens and a new earth; the past events will not be remembered or come to mind."

Is 65:17

"For just as the new heavens and the new earth, which I will make, will remain before me"— this is the LORD's declaration— "so your offspring and your name will remain."

Is 66:22

"All kinds of trees providing food will grow along both banks of the river. Their leaves will not wither, and their fruit will not fail. Each month they will bear fresh fruit because the water comes from the sanctuary. Their fruit will be used for eating and their leaves for healing."

Ezk 47:12

ALLEGIANCE TO THE KING

Day 17

As followers of Jesus, our allegiance is to the King, and His kingdom is our priority. Submitting to Christ as King is an act of worship.

Deuteronomy 6:4–5

[4] "Listen, Israel: The LORD our God, the LORD is one. [5] Love the LORD your God with all your heart, with all your soul, and with all your strength."

Luke 9:21–27

HIS DEATH AND RESURRECTION PREDICTED

[21] But he strictly warned and instructed them to tell this to no one, [22] saying, "It is necessary that the Son of Man suffer many things and be rejected by the elders, chief priests, and scribes, be killed, and be raised the third day."

TAKE UP YOUR CROSS

[23] Then he said to them all,

"If anyone wants to follow after me, let him deny himself, take up his cross daily, and follow me.

[24] For whoever wants to save his life will lose it, but whoever loses his life because of me will save it. [25] For what does it benefit someone if he gains the whole world, and yet loses or forfeits himself? [26] For whoever is ashamed of me and my words, the Son of Man will be ashamed of him when he comes in his glory and that of the Father and the holy angels. [27] Truly I tell you, there are some standing here who will not taste death until they see the kingdom of God."

Luke 18:18–30

THE RICH YOUNG RULER

[18] A ruler asked him, "Good teacher, what must I do to inherit eternal life?"

[19] "Why do you call me good?" Jesus asked him. "No one is good except God alone. [20] You know the commandments: Do not commit adultery; do not murder; do not steal; do not bear false witness; honor your father and mother."

[21] "I have kept all these from my youth," he said.

[22] When Jesus heard this, he told him, "You still lack one thing: Sell all you have and distribute it to the poor, and you will have treasure in heaven. Then come, follow me."

²³ After he heard this, he became extremely sad, because he was very rich.

POSSESSIONS AND THE KINGDOM

²⁴ Seeing that he became sad, Jesus said, "How hard it is for those who have wealth to enter the kingdom of God! ²⁵ For it is easier for a camel to go through the eye of a needle than for a rich person to enter the kingdom of God."

²⁶ Those who heard this asked, "Then who can be saved?"

²⁷ He replied, "What is impossible with man is possible with God."

²⁸ Then Peter said, "Look, we have left what we had and followed you."

²⁹ So he said to them, "Truly I tell you, there is no one who has left a house, wife or brothers or sisters, parents or children because of the kingdom of God, ³⁰ who will not receive many times more at this time, and eternal life in the age to come."

Philippians 3:20–21

²⁰ Our citizenship is in heaven, and we eagerly wait for a Savior from there, the Lord Jesus Christ.

²¹ He will transform the body of our humble condition into the likeness of his glorious body, by the power that enables him to subject everything to himself.

1 John 2:15–17

A WARNING ABOUT THE WORLD

¹⁵ Do not love the world or the things in the world. If anyone loves the world, the love of the Father is not in him. ¹⁶ For everything in the world—the lust of the flesh, the lust of the eyes, and the pride in one's possessions—is not from the Father, but is from the world. ¹⁷ And the world with its lust is passing away, but the one who does the will of God remains forever.

Day 17

REFLECTION

What does it look like to make the kingdom of God your priority?
What keeps you from doing so?

QUESTIONS

Identify a situation in your life where God's Spirit may be leading you to practice submission. What steps of obedience can you take as an act of submission?

AND HE SHALL REIGN FOREVER AND EVER.

KING OF KINGS, LORD OF LORDS.

Handel's *Messiah*: "Hallelujah Chorus"

ADVANCING THE KINGDOM

Our King calls us to share in His kingdom
work and participate in its growth.

Day 18

Matthew 13:1–23, 31–32

THE PARABLE OF THE SOWER

¹ On that day Jesus went out of the house and was sitting by the sea.
² Such large crowds gathered around him that he got into a boat and
sat down, while the whole crowd stood on the shore.

³ Then he told them many things in parables, saying, "Consider the
sower who went out to sow. ⁴ As he sowed, some seed fell along the
path, and the birds came and devoured them. ⁵ Other seed fell on
rocky ground where it didn't have much soil, and it grew up quickly
since the soil wasn't deep. ⁶ But when the sun came up, it was scorched,
and since it had no root, it withered away. ⁷ Other seed fell among
thorns, and the thorns came up and choked it. ⁸ Still other seed fell
on good ground and produced fruit: some a hundred, some sixty, and
some thirty times what was sown. ⁹ Let anyone who has ears listen."

WHY JESUS USED PARABLES

¹⁰ Then the disciples came up and asked him, "Why are you speaking
to them in parables?"

¹¹ He answered, "Because the secrets of the kingdom of heaven have
been given for you to know, but it has not been given to them. ¹² For
whoever has, more will be given to him, and he will have more than
enough; but whoever does not have, even what he has will be taken
away from him. ¹³ That is why I speak to them in parables, because
looking they do not see, and hearing they do not listen or understand.
¹⁴ Isaiah's prophecy is fulfilled in them, which says:

You will listen and listen,
but never understand;
you will look and look,
but never perceive.
¹⁵ For this people's heart has grown callous;
their ears are hard of hearing,
and they have shut their eyes;
otherwise they might see with their eyes,
and hear with their ears, and

understand with their hearts,
and turn back—
and I would heal them.

[16] "Blessed are your eyes because they do see, and your ears because they do hear. [17] For truly I tell you, many prophets and righteous people longed to see the things you see but didn't see them, to hear the things you hear but didn't hear them.

THE PARABLE OF THE SOWER EXPLAINED

[18] "So listen to the parable of the sower: [19] When anyone hears the word about the kingdom and doesn't understand it, the evil one comes and snatches away what was sown in his heart. This is the one sown along the path. [20] And the one sown on rocky ground—this is one who hears the word and immediately receives it with joy. [21] But he has no root and is short-lived. When distress or persecution comes because of the word, immediately he falls away. [22] Now the one sown among the thorns—this is one who hears the word, but the worries of this age and the deceitfulness of wealth choke the word, and it becomes unfruitful. [23] But the one sown on the good ground—this is one who hears and understands the word, who does produce fruit and yields: some a hundred, some sixty, some thirty times what was sown."

…

THE PARABLES OF THE MUSTARD SEED AND OF THE LEAVEN

[31] He presented another parable to them: "The kingdom of heaven is like a mustard seed that a man took and sowed in his field. [32] It's the smallest of all the seeds, but when grown, it's taller than the garden plants and becomes a tree, so that the birds of the sky come and nest in its branches."

Matthew 28:16–20

THE GREAT COMMISSION

[16] The eleven disciples traveled to Galilee, to the mountain where Jesus had directed them. [17] When they saw him, they worshiped, but some doubted. [18] Jesus came near and said to them, "All authority has been given to me in heaven and on earth. [19] Go, therefore, and make disciples of all nations, baptizing them in the name of the Father and of the Son and of the Holy Spirit, [20] teaching them to observe everything I have commanded you. And remember, I am with you always, to the end of the age."

Ephesians 4:4–14

⁴ There is one body and one Spirit—just as you were called to one hope at your calling— ⁵ one Lord, one faith, one baptism, ⁶ one God and Father of all, who is above all and through all and in all.

⁷ Now grace was given to each one of us according to the measure of Christ's gift. ⁸ For it says:

> When he ascended on high,
> he took the captives captive;
> he gave gifts to people.

⁹ But what does "he ascended" mean except that he also descended to the lower parts of the earth? ¹⁰ The one who descended is also the one who ascended far above all the heavens, to fill all things. ¹¹ And he himself gave some to be apostles, some prophets, some evangelists, some pastors and teachers, ¹² to equip the saints for the work of ministry, to build up the body of Christ, ¹³ until we all reach unity in the faith and in the knowledge of God's Son, growing into maturity with a stature measured by Christ's fullness. ¹⁴ Then we will no longer be little children, tossed by the waves and blown around by every wind of teaching, by human cunning with cleverness in the techniques of deceit.

James 5:7–8

WAITING FOR THE LORD

⁷ Therefore, brothers and sisters, be patient until the Lord's coming. See how the farmer waits for the precious fruit of the earth and is patient with it until it receives the early and the late rains. ⁸ You also must be patient. Strengthen your hearts, because the Lord's coming is near.

1 Peter 2:11–12

A CALL TO GOOD WORKS

¹¹ Dear friends, I urge you as strangers and exiles to abstain from sinful desires that wage war against the soul. ¹² Conduct yourselves honorably among the Gentiles, so that when they slander you as evildoers, they will observe your good works and will glorify God on the day he visits.

Day 18

REFLECTION

What are some unique ways God has gifted and equipped
you to take part in kingdom work?

QUESTIONS

Who has encouraged you in advancing the kingdom? Who can
you encourage to persevere in their own kingdom work?

Jesus's return will usher in a spiritual and physical reality in which the heavens and earth are fully renewed, where He reigns as faithful King with His redeemed people forever.

THE FULLNESS OF THE KINGDOM

Psalm 46

GOD OUR REFUGE

For the choir director. A song of the sons of Korah. According to Alamoth.

¹ God is our refuge and strength,
a helper who is always found
in times of trouble.
² Therefore we will not be afraid,
though the earth trembles
and the mountains topple
into the depths of the seas,
³ though its water roars and foams
and the mountains quake with its turmoil.   *Selah*

⁴ There is a river—
its streams delight the city of God,
the holy dwelling place of the Most High.
⁵ God is within her; she will not be toppled.
God will help her when the morning dawns.
⁶ Nations rage, kingdoms topple;
the earth melts when he lifts his voice.
⁷ The LORD of Armies is with us;
the God of Jacob is our stronghold.   *Selah*

⁸ Come, see the works of the LORD,
who brings devastation on the earth.
⁹ He makes wars cease throughout the earth.
He shatters bows and cuts spears to pieces;
he sets wagons ablaze.
¹⁰ "Stop fighting, and know that I am God,
exalted among the nations, exalted on
the earth."
¹¹ The LORD of Armies is with us;
the God of Jacob is our stronghold.   *Selah*

1 Corinthians 15:51–57

⁵¹ Behold, I am telling you a mystery; we will not all sleep, but we will all be changed, ⁵² in a moment, in the twinkling of an eye, at the last trumpet; for the trumpet will sound, and the dead will be raised imperishable, and we will be changed. ⁵³ For this perishable must put on the imperishable, and this mortal must

put on immortality. ⁵⁴ But when this perishable puts on the imperishable, and this mortal puts on immortality, then will come about the saying that is written: "Death has been swallowed up in victory. ⁵⁵ Where, O Death, is your victory? Where, O Death, is your sting?" ⁵⁶ The sting of death is sin, and the power of sin is the Law; ⁵⁷ but thanks be to God, who gives us the victory through our Lord Jesus Christ.

1 Thessalonians 4:13–18
THE COMFORT OF CHRIST'S COMING

¹³ We do not want you to be uninformed, brothers and sisters, concerning those who are asleep, so that you will not grieve like the rest, who have no hope. ¹⁴ For if we believe that Jesus died and rose again, in the same way, through Jesus, God will bring with him those who have fallen asleep. ¹⁵ For we say this to you by a word from the Lord: We who are still alive at the Lord's coming will certainly not precede those who have fallen asleep. ¹⁶ For the Lord himself will descend from heaven with a shout, with the archangel's voice, and with the trumpet of God, and the dead in Christ will rise first. ¹⁷ Then we who are still alive, who are left, will be caught up together with them in the clouds to meet the Lord in the air, and so we will always be with the Lord. ¹⁸ Therefore encourage one another with these words.

Revelation 22
THE SOURCE OF LIFE

¹ Then he showed me the river of the water of life, clear as crystal, flowing from the throne of God and of the Lamb ² down the middle of the city's main street. The tree of life was on each side of the river, bearing twelve kinds of fruit, producing its fruit every month. The leaves of the tree are for healing the nations, ³ and there will no longer be any curse. The throne of God and of the Lamb will be in the city, and his servants will worship him. ⁴ They will see his face, and his name will be on their foreheads.

⁵ Night will be no more; people will not need the light of a lamp or the light of the sun, because the Lord God will give them light, and they will reign forever and ever.

THE TIME IS NEAR

⁶ Then he said to me, "These words are faithful and true. The Lord, the God of the spirits of the prophets, has sent his angel to show his servants what must soon take place."

[7] "Look, I am coming soon! Blessed is the one who keeps the words of the prophecy of this book."

[8] I, John, am the one who heard and saw these things. When I heard and saw them, I fell down to worship at the feet of the angel who had shown them to me. [9] But he said to me, "Don't do that! I am a fellow servant with you, your brothers the prophets, and those who keep the words of this book. Worship God!"

[10] Then he said to me, "Don't seal up the words of the prophecy of this book, because the time is near. [11] Let the unrighteous go on in unrighteousness; let the filthy still be filthy; let the righteous go on in righteousness; let the holy still be holy."

[12] "Look, I am coming soon, and my reward is with me to repay each person according to his work.

[13] I am the Alpha and the Omega, the first and the last, the beginning and the end.

[14] "Blessed are those who wash their robes, so that they may have the right to the tree of life and may enter the city by the gates. [15] Outside are the dogs, the sorcerers, the sexually immoral, the murderers, the idolaters, and everyone who loves and practices falsehood.

[16] "I, Jesus, have sent my angel to attest these things to you for the churches. I am the Root and descendant of David, the bright morning star."

[17] Both the Spirit and the bride say, "Come!" Let anyone who hears, say, "Come!" Let the one who is thirsty come. Let the one who desires take the water of life freely.

[18] I testify to everyone who hears the words of the prophecy of this book: If anyone adds to them, God will add to him the plagues that are written in this book. [19] And if anyone takes away from the words of the book of this prophecy, God will take away his share of the tree of life and the holy city, which are written about in this book.

[20] He who testifies about these things says, "Yes, I am coming soon."

Amen! Come, Lord Jesus!

[21] The grace of the Lord Jesus be with everyone. Amen.

Day 19

REFLECTION

How does fellowship with other believers help you
anticipate the coming fullness of the kingdom?

QUESTIONS

Throughout this reading plan, how has your knowledge of the
kingdom of God expanded or changed? What is the most exciting or
interesting thing you learned?

GRACE

Take this day to catch up on your reading, pray,
and rest in the presence of the Lord.

Day 20

DAY

Our citizenship is in heaven, and we eagerly wait for a Savior from there, the Lord Jesus Christ. He will transform the body of our humble condition into the likeness of his glorious body, by the power that enables him to subject everything to himself.

Philippians 3:20-21

WEEKLY

Scripture is God-breathed and true. When we memorize it, we
carry the good news of Jesus with us wherever we go.

We are memorizing the Lord's Prayer together. The third part of the
prayer asks God to guide us away from temptation and evil, so that
we might walk toward His grace and love. The last line exalts God
as infinite, omnipotent, and eternal.

Day 21

TRUTH

"Our Father which art in heaven, Hallowed be thy name.
Thy kingdom come, Thy will be done in earth, as it is in heaven.
Give us this day our daily bread.
And forgive us our debts, as we forgive our debtors.
And lead us not into temptation, but deliver us from evil: For thine
is the kingdom, and the power, and the glory, for ever. Amen."

Matthew 6:9-13 KJV

Benediction

THY
KINGDOM
COME.
THY WILL

BE DONE IN EARTH. AS IT IS IN HEAVEN.

Matthew 6:10 KJV

CSB BOOK ABBREVIATIONS

OLD TESTAMENT

GN Genesis

EX Exodus

LV Leviticus

NM Numbers

DT Deuteronomy

JOS Joshua

JDG Judges

RU Ruth

1SM 1 Samuel

2SM 2 Samuel

1KG 1 Kings

2KG 2 Kings

1CH 1 Chronicles

2CH 2 Chronicles

EZR Ezra

NEH Nehemiah

EST Esther

JB Job

PS Psalms

PR Proverbs

EC Ecclesiastes

SG Song of Solomon

IS Isaiah

JR Jeremiah

LM Lamentations

EZK Ezekiel

DN Daniel

HS Hosea

JL Joel

AM Amos

OB Obadiah

JNH Jonah

MC Micah

NAH Nahum

HAB Habakkuk

ZPH Zephaniah

HG Haggai

ZCH Zechariah

MAL Malachi

NEW TESTAMENT

MT Matthew

MK Mark

LK Luke

JN John

AC Acts

RM Romans

1CO 1 Corinthians

2CO 2 Corinthians

GL Galatians

EPH Ephesians

PHP Philippians

COL Colossians

1TH 1 Thessalonians

2TH 2 Thessalonians

1TM 1 Timothy

2TM 2 Timothy

TI Titus

PHM Philemon

HEB Hebrews

JMS James

1PT 1 Peter

2PT 2 Peter

1JN 1 John

2JN 2 John

3JN 3 John

JD Jude

RV Revelation

SHE READS TRUTH
PODCAST

God's Word is for you and for now.

Join our founders Raechel and Amanda in conversation that delights in the beauty, goodness, and truth found in Scripture. Created to complement the current community reading plan, the She Reads Truth podcast will encourage you on your commute to work, while you're out for a walk, or at home making dinner. Subscribe today and don't miss an episode!

JOIN US ON APPLE PODCASTS OR YOUR PREFERRED STREAMING PLATFORM

WHERE DID I STUDY?

O HOME
O OFFICE
O COFFEE SHOP
O CHURCH
O A FRIEND'S HOUSE
O OTHER:

WHAT WAS I LISTENING TO?

ARTIST:

SONG:

PLAYLIST:

WHEN DID I STUDY?

MORNING

AFTERNOON

NIGHT

HOW DID I FIND DELIGHT IN GOD'S WORD?

WHAT WAS HAPPENING IN MY LIFE?

WHAT WAS HAPPENING IN THE WORLD?

MONTH	DAY	YEAR

END DATE